Reading Essentials in Science

THE MATERIAL WORLD

Classifying/Grouping Materials

LEWIS PARKER

PERFECTION LEARNING®

What is matter?

Editorial Director:	Susan C. Thies
Editor:	Lori A. Meyer
Design Director:	Randy Messer
Book Design:	Michelle Glass
Cover Design:	Michael A. Aspengren

Dedication

This book is dedicated to my family,
especially to Dakota, Tyrus, and Nicholas.

Acknowledgements

A special thanks to the following for his scientific review of the book:
Kris Mandsager, Instructor of Physics and Astronomy,
North Iowa Area Community College, Mason City, IA

Image Credits: © Tim McGuire/CORBIS: p. 10 (right), © Richard Cummins/CORBIS: p. 11; © Roger Ressmeyer/CORBIS: p. 21

© Royalty-Free/CORBIS: pp. 10 (left), 13, 17 (right), 18 (left); Photos.com: top and bottom backgrounds, pp. 8 (right), 12, 14, 15 (left), 16, 17 (left), 18, 19, 23; Ingram Publishing: pp. 3, 4, 5, 6, 7 (right), 8 (left), 20, 24; Perfection Learning Corporation: pp. 7 (left), 9, 15 (center and right)

Front cover (left to right): Ingram, Perfection Learning Corporation, Corel, Photos.com, Photos.com, Perfection Learning Corporation, Corel (background); Back cover: Corel

Text © 2006 by Perfection Learning® Corporation.
All rights reserved. No part of this book may be
reproduced, stored in a retrieval system, or
transmitted in any form or by any means, electronic,
mechanical, photocopying, recording, or otherwise,
without prior permission of the publisher.
Printed in the United States of America.

For information, contact
Perfection Learning® Corporation
1000 North Second Avenue, P.O. Box 500
Logan, Iowa 51546-0500.
Phone: 1-800-831-4190
Fax: 1-800-543-2745
perfectionlearning.com

1 2 3 4 5 6 PP 10 09 08 07 06 05

Paperback ISBN 0-7891-6637-2
Reinforced Library Binding ISBN 0-7569-4698-0

Table of Contents

1. What Is Matter? 4
2. What State Is It In? 6
3. What Are the Basic Properties? 11
4. What Does It Weigh and What Size Is It?. 16
5. What Is Its Temperature? 18
6. What Is It Made Of? 20

   Internet Connections and Related Reading
   for Classifying/Grouping Materials 22

   Glossary 23

   Index 24

What Is Matter?

Matter is a word that describes all the objects and materials on Earth. The air you breathe is matter. The water you drink is matter. The food you eat is matter. The paper and pencil that you use to do your homework are matter. Your house is matter. In fact, you are matter too.

Everything you can see and touch is matter—an apple, a coat, a box. And many things that you cannot see or touch are also matter—the air you breathe, for instance. Matter is everything that is living—all the plants and animals. Matter is also everything that is not alive—rocks and socks, for example.

Mass and Volume

All matter has two things in common. All matter has **mass**. Mass is how much matter an object contains.

All matter also has **volume**. When we speak of the volume of an object, we are talking about how much space it takes up. Does a pencil have mass? Yes. Does it have volume? Yes. So a pencil is matter.

Solid, Liquid, or Gas?

Matter can be classified in different ways. An easy way to classify matter is according to what state or form it is in. Matter can usually be grouped as a **solid**, **liquid**, or **gas**.

Matter can also be classified according to its characteristics or properties. A property of

A pencil is matter.

matter is something that you can observe about the matter without changing it. Different kinds of matter have different properties. You observe these properties through your senses. You can see, touch, smell, or feel the different properties of matter—color, shape, size, flexibility, hardness, or texture.

Classifying matter helps us understand the materials and objects that make up our world and how they can be used to make our lives better.

Matter is everything.

5

What is matter?

What State Is It In?

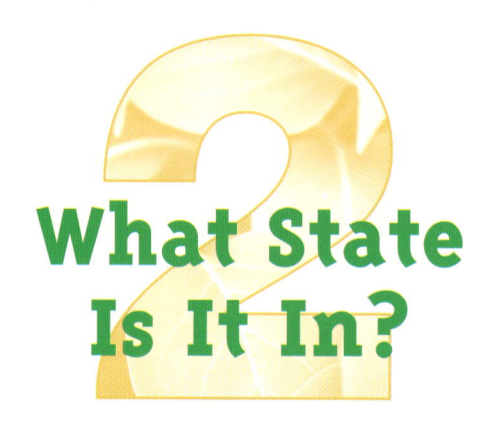

One way to classify matter is to decide what form it is in. These forms are called *states*. Almost all matter can be classified in a solid, liquid, or gas state. Each of these states of matter has its own characteristics, or properties.

Solids

You see, touch, smell, and feel solids all the time. The book you hold in your hands is a solid. A doughnut is a solid. Your computer is a solid.

All solids are alike in particular ways. Solids have a fixed shape. They keep their shape unless something acts on them. Your pencil will always look like a pencil unless you break it.

6

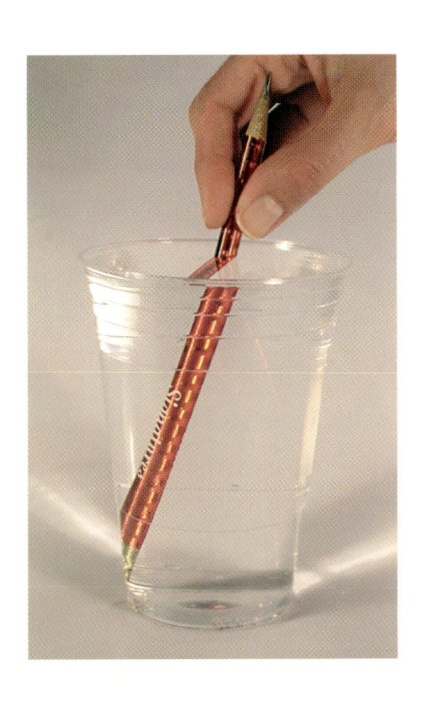

Solids also keep their volume. To measure the volume of a pencil, you can see how much water is displaced when the pencil is submerged in a glass of water. If you break the pencil into pieces and then submerge the pieces in water, the same amount of water is displaced from the glass as with the unbroken pencil.

Liquids

Pour yourself a glass of milk. Notice that the milk takes on the same shape as the glass you poured it in. If you spill the milk, the shape of the milk will change. Now pour the milk into a glass that is a different shape. The shape of the milk changes again. But the mass and volume of the milk stay the same.

Liquids do not have a fixed shape. A liquid takes the shape of its container. But a liquid has a definite volume. It always takes up the same amount of space, no matter what container it is poured into.

What is matter?

A balloon is filled with gases.

Gases

Take a deep breath of air. You just inhaled several gases—mostly nitrogen and oxygen—into your lungs. You didn't see these gases, and you couldn't feel them. If the air was fresh and clean, you could not smell the gases either.

Gases do not have a fixed shape. They take the shape of the container that they go into. If you heat a gas, cool it, or squash it, you change how much space it fits into. A gas can also flow. It can move from one place to another to fill up the space. The air from the balloon could be pumped into a rectangular box and take its shape. Objects easily pass through most gases. When you walk around, you pass through air. You can feel breezes and winds because gases have mass.

Chlorine is used in swimming pools.

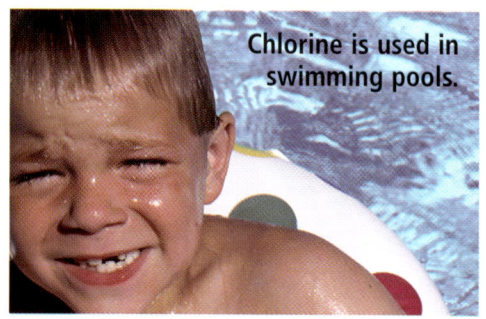

You cannot see most gases, but you can smell and see some. Sulphur dioxide is a gas that stinks like rotten eggs. Chlorine is a green gas. It is often put into swimming pool water to kill germs.

Inquire and Investigate: Cooling a Gas

Question: What happens when a gas is cooled?

Answer the Question: I think a gas will _____ when cooled.

Form a hypothesis: If a gas is cooled, it will _____.

Test the hypothesis:

Materials:
- large balloon (a 10-inch balloon would work)
- cloth tape measure
- freezer (use the freezer part of your refrigerator if the balloon will fit inside)
- paper and pencil

Procedure:
1. Blow up the balloon and tie it off so the air does not escape.
2. Measure the circumference of the balloon. The circumference is the distance around the balloon at its middle. Record the circumference on the paper. Label this measurement as "Room Temperature Measurement Number 1."
3. Place the balloon in the freezer for 24 hours.
4. After 24 hours, take the balloon out of the freezer and measure the circumference again. Record the balloon's circumference on your paper. Label this measurement as "Freezer Measurement."
5. Keep the balloon out of the freezer until it warms up to the temperature of the room.
6. Measure the circumference again and record your findings as "Room Temperature Measurement Number 2." Compare your measurements.

Observation: The balloon's circumference was smallest when you took it out of the freezer. It shrunk while it was in the freezer but returned to its normal size once it warmed to room temperature.

Conclusion: Cooling a gas makes it shrink or decrease in volume. A gas expands when it is heated.

What is matter?

Changing from One State to Another

Matter can be changed from one state to another, and these changes happen all the time. A popsicle is solid matter when you take it out of the freezer to eat it. If you hold it too long on a hot day, it will melt and turn into liquid matter. Put the melting popsicle back into the freezer, and it returns to being solid matter. Water is a solid when it is ice. It is a liquid as water and a gas when it changes to steam.

Heat is all it takes to move matter from being a solid to a liquid or to a gas. When liquid matter is cooled to its **freezing point**, continuing to remove heat causes it to change to solid matter. When solid matter is heated to its **melting point**, continued heating causes it to become liquid matter. If you heat up liquid matter to its **boiling point**, it changes into gaseous matter.

Water at boiling point

What Are the Basic Properties?

You can classify objects according to their basic properties. These are properties that you can observe through your senses. You do not have to weigh an object or measure it to observe how an object looks, feels, or acts. Brittleness, color, conductivity, elasticity, hardness, magnetism, shape, and texture are basic properties.

Brittleness

Brittleness is a property of solids. Materials are described as brittle if they crack or break easily. A china plate is hard, but it will break into pieces if you drop it.

Glass is brittle.

What is matter?

Scientists test for brittleness by tapping an object with a hammer. Some materials become brittle when they are placed in extremely cold temperatures. You can stretch a balloon because it is made out of an elastic material called *rubber*. But if you place the balloon in a bowl of liquid nitrogen, the balloon will not stretch. At room temperature, nitrogen is a gas, but when it is cooled far below zero degrees Fahrenheit, it becomes liquid. The liquid nitrogen causes the rubber balloon to become so brittle that it shatters into pieces when you stretch it.

Color

Color is another basic property scientists use to classify objects. When you look at an apple, you know whether it is red, yellow, or green. You can observe the color property of the apples. You can place all the red apples in one classification and the yellow and green apples in two other classifications.

Luster is another property that is similar to color. Luster refers to whether an object is shiny or dull. A bright brass bell has high luster because it is shiny. An old, rusty spoon has low luster because it is dull.

Feathers act as an insulator to keep the parrot warm.

Conductivity

Conductivity means that a solid object can carry heat or electricity through it. Cooking pans have conductivity. They are usually made of a metal that can conduct, or carry, the heat from the oven or fire to the food that will be baked or cooked.

Objects that do not have good conductivity are called *insulators*. Feathers are a good insulator, which is why birds stay warm. That's also why you stay warm in your down jacket. Glass and air are also good insulators.

Elasticity

Some objects can be classified by how well they stretch, or how elastic they are. Rubber is a well-known elastic material. You can stretch a rubber band. When you let go, it shrinks back to its original shape.

Other materials that you would not think of are also elastic. For example, steel is an elastic metal. That's why it is used to make bridges and other structures exposed to changes in temperature. The steel expands in heat and contracts when it's cold. However, steel will only stretch so far before it will not return to its original shape and size.

What is matter?

Hardness

Hardness is another property that is used to classify solid objects. Solid materials are classified as hard, medium hard, or soft. A stick of butter, a block of wood, and a lump of clay are all solids. But their hardnesses are quite different.

The hardest natural substance is a diamond. Only another diamond can scratch it. Aluminum is a soft metal, but that doesn't mean it isn't useful. You drink soda from aluminum cans, and aluminum lines carry electricity into your home.

Magnetism

Some objects made from iron, steel, or nickel have a property called *magnetism*. That means that they are attracted by magnets. Sometimes these metals can even be turned into magnets.

Shape

Shape is another basic property of matter. But what shape does matter come in? That's an easy question to answer—all shapes. But only solid objects have shapes. A ball is solid matter that is round. A block is solid matter that is square or cubed. Some solid matter may be in shapes that range from rectangles to pentagons. The shapes may be curved or flat.

Tire    **Cotton balls**    **Sandpaper**

Texture

Objects may be classified according to their texture. Some solid objects are soft to the touch, like cotton balls. Others may be rough like a wad of steel wool. Objects may also be classified as smooth, bumpy, or scratchy. A mirror is a smooth object. A bike tire has a bumpy texture. Sandpaper and nail files have rough or scratchy textures. Baby powder has a powdery texture.

Liquids can be classified according to whether they are thick or thin. Milk is a thin liquid object compared to molasses, which is thick. Liquids like clean water may also appear transparent in texture, so you can see through them. Chocolate milk has an **opaque** texture, which means you can't see through it.

What is matter?

4 What Does It Weigh and What Size Is It?

Elephants are very heavy.

You can classify objects by how much they weigh and by their size. Both of these properties can be measured. How strongly the Earth attracts an object is its weight. Some objects such as feathers are very light. Other objects such as elephants are very heavy. But an object does not have to be huge to weigh a lot. A small bar of lead can be hard to lift. Weight is dependent on what material the object is made of and how much of the material makes it up.

moves on the scale to show the weight of the object.

When you go to a doctor's office, a nurse will use a balance to find out how much you weigh. The nurse moves the weights across the top of the balance until the pointer is on the balance point. Then the numbers on the balance measure your weight.

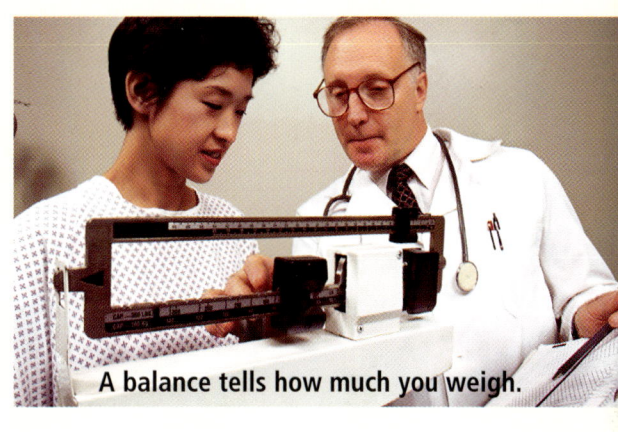

A balance tells how much you weigh.

Scales and Balances

You can measure the weight of solid objects by using scales or balances. You have probably seen a scale in the fruits and vegetables section of a supermarket. You can place fruit on the scale to find out how much it weighs. The scale usually contains a spring. When an object is placed on the scale, the spring is squished down or stretched out depending on how heavy the object is. A pointer attached to the end of the spring

Size

You can classify objects into groups according to their size too. Some objects, like a giraffe, are large. Other objects are so tiny that you need a microscope to see them. You can use a tape measure or a ruler to measure the length, width, and height of objects and put them into groups.

What Is Its Temperature?

You can classify objects by their temperature. Scientists use thermometers to measure temperature. The two commonly used temperature scales are Fahrenheit and Celsius. On the Fahrenheit thermometer, water freezes at 32 degrees and boils at 212 degrees. On the Celsius thermometer, water freezes at 0 degrees and boils at 100 degrees.

Freezing, Melting, and Boiling Temperatures

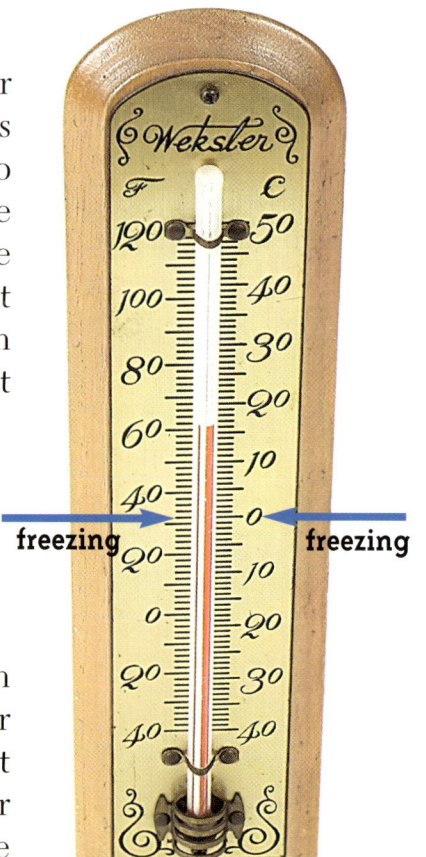

Objects can change their state when they reach their freezing temperature or melting temperature. Water in a glass at room temperature is a liquid. If you pour water into a tray and place it in the freezer, the liquid water will freeze into a solid called *ice*. The freezer temperature must be no higher than 32 degrees Fahrenheit or 0 degrees Celsius. If you place the ice in a pan and set it on a stove with heat above 212 degrees Fahrenheit or 100 degrees Celsius, the ice will first melt into a liquid. Then the liquid warms to the boiling temperature, and the boiling water turns into a gas called *steam*.

Almost every material has a particular melting and freezing temperature. But those temperatures vary for different materials. For example, iron must reach a high temperature to change from solid to liquid. Iron is usually placed in a very hot furnace to melt it. Then the iron becomes a glowing, yellow liquid. If the liquid iron were placed on the Sun, it would get hot enough to boil and change into a gas.

The melting point of a solid is the same as the freezing point of its liquid. This means that ice melts to water at the same temperature that water freezes to ice. The boiling point is when a liquid changes into gas or a gas changes into a liquid. The boiling point is always higher than the melting point.

Melting iron

Scientist of Significance

Anders Celsius (1701–1744) was born in Sweden. He came from a family of scientists. As a young man, Celsius was interested in the stars and planets. At age 29, he became a professor of astronomy. As an astronomer, Celsius was able to calculate the brightness of 300 stars. He developed the Celsius temperature scale based on the freezing and boiling temperatures of water.

What is matter?

6 What Is It Made Of?

You can classify objects according to what they are made of. Objects can be made of wood, metal, clay, cloth, or paper—but that's just the start. In fact, there are actually about 300,000 different materials, and scientists continue to combine these materials in new ways. So the number of materials is increasing all the time.

Nature or Human?

You can group objects that are made of materials that come from nature. A chair is made of wood. The wood came from a tree. A cotton shirt is made of cotton. The cotton came from plants that grew in the ground.

You can group other objects that have materials made by humans. A fork that you use on a picnic is made of plastic. Plastic is a human-made material. Steel is used to make cars. Steel is a human-made material.

One Material or Two?

You can classify objects as to whether they are made up of only one kind of material or of many materials. Copper and silver are **elements**, which are substances made up of one kind of material. Glass is made by melting together sand, lime, and soda. Salt is made of two elements—sodium and chlorine. Water is made up of two gases—hydrogen and oxygen.

Matter is everything you can see, feel, touch, and smell—living and nonliving. Adding or removing heat can change matter from one state to another. You can classify matter using its characteristics or properties. Some basic properties can be observed while others need to be measured. Whether you are classifying it, measuring it, or observing it, matter matters!

Technology Link: A Cosmic Catcher

Aerogel is the lightest known material. A block of aerogel the size of a six-foot person weighs about one pound. It is light, but it can hold 500 to 4000 times its weight. Aerogel is usually transparent with a blue tint and is often called *frozen smoke*. Aerogel is made from silica, a mineral found in sand.

Aerogel is used by the United States space program. Some spacecraft exploring far out in the Solar System have nets made of aerogel. These nets are used to catch dust from comets. Space suits made of aerogel are also now being developed.

Internet Connections and Related Reading for Classifying/Grouping Materials

http://www.primaryresources.co.uk/science/science3.htm
This site has many resources for grouping and classifying materials.

http://www.chem4kids.com/files/matter_intro.html
Explore matter and its states with this site.

http://www.cdli.ca/CITE/matter.htm
This site is all about matter and has quizzes to try.

http://www.apqj64.dsl.pipex.com/sfa/slg.htm
This Science for All site tells about solids, liquids, and gases.

* * * * * * * * * * *

Magnetism by Ben Morgan. Learn more about magnets and magnetism. Blackbirch Press, 2004. [RL 3 IL 2–5] (6876106 HB)

Matter: See It, Touch It, Taste It, Smell It by Darlene Stille. Learn more about matter. Picture Window Books, 2004. [RL 2 IL K–4] (3514706 HB)

Solid, Liquid, or Gas? by Allan Fowler. Explore solids, liquids, and gases. Children's Press, 1995. [RL 2.8 IL K–3] (3794606 HB)

Temperature: Heating Up and Cooling Down by Darlene Stille. Take a look at how things heat up and cool down. Picture Window Books, 2004. [RL 2 IL K–4] (3514906 HB)

What Is the World Made Of? All About Solids, Liquids, and Gases by Kathleen Weidner Zoehfeld. Introduces readers to the differences between solids, liquids, and gases. Harper Collins, 1998. [RL 3 IL K–3] (5668801 PB 5668802 CC)

- RL = Reading Level
- IL = Interest Level

Perfection Learning's catalog numbers are included for your ordering convenience. PB indicates paperback. HB indicates hardback. CC indicates Cover Craft.

Glossary

boiling point
(BOYL ing poynt) temperature at which a liquid turns to gas

element
(EHL uh ment) any of more than 100 substances that are made up of one kind of material

freezing point
(FREEZ ing poynt) temperature at which a liquid becomes solid

gas
(gas) matter that is spread out and has changed shape and volume

liquid
(LIK wid) matter that keeps its volume but changes shape to fit its container

mass
(mas) amount of matter an object contains

melting point
(MELT ing poynt) temperature at which a solid melts

opaque
(oh PAYK) not allowing passage of light, so that images cannot be seen through it

solid
(SAWL id) matter that keeps the same shape and volume

volume
(VAWL youm) total amount of something; how much space something takes up

Matter is everything!

Index

aerogel, 21
aluminum, 14
balance, 17
boiling point, 10
brittleness, 11–12
Celsius, Anders, 19
chlorine, 8, 21
color, 12
conductivity, 13
cotton, 15, 20
diamond, 14
elasticity, 13
element, 21
Fahrenheit, 18, 19
freezing point, 10, 18
gases, 5, 8, 9
    nitrogen, 8, 12, 21
    oxygen, 8, 21
hardness, 14
insulator, 13
liquids, 5, 7
luster, 12

magnetism, 14
melting point, 10, 19
rubber, 12
scale, 17
shape, 14
size, 17
sodium, 21
solids, 5, 6–7
states, 6–10
steel, 13, 20
temperature, 18–19
texture, 15
wood, 20